The Treasure in Earthen Vessels

Living Stream Ministry
Anaheim, CA • www.lsm.org

ISBN 978-1-57593-860-8

Living Stream Ministry
2431 W. La Palma Ave., Anaheim, CA 92801
P. O. Box 2121, Anaheim, CA 92814 USA

Printed in India

10 11 12 13 14 / 8 7 6 5 4 3

THE TREASURE IN EARTHEN VESSELS

"For we do not want you to be ignorant, brothers, of our affliction which befell us in Asia, that we were excessively burdened, beyond our power, so that we despaired even of living. Indeed we ourselves had the response of death in ourselves, that we should not base our confidence on ourselves but on God, who raises the dead" (2 Cor. 1:8-9).

"This therefore intending, did I then use fickleness? Or the things which I purpose, do I purpose according to the flesh, so that with me there should be Yes, yes and No, no?" (v. 17).

"For if I cause you sorrow…" (2:2a).

"And I wrote this very thing to you" (v. 3a).

"For out of much affliction and anguish of heart I wrote to you through many tears, not that you would be made sorrowful but that you would know the love

which I have more abundantly toward you"
(v. 4).

"Are we beginning again to commend
ourselves? Or do we need, as some do, letters of commendation to you or from you?"
(3:1).

"Not that we are sufficient of ourselves
to account anything as from ourselves; but
our sufficiency is from God" (v. 5).

"But we have this treasure in earthen
vessels that the excellency of the power
may be of God and not out of us. We are
pressed on every side but not constricted;
unable to find a way out but not utterly
without a way out; persecuted but not
abandoned; cast down but not destroyed;
always bearing about in the body the putting to death of Jesus that the life of Jesus
also may be manifested in our body"
(4:7-10).

"For also, we who are in this tabernacle
groan, being burdened, in that we do not
desire to be unclothed, but clothed upon,
that what is mortal may be swallowed up
by life" (5:4).

"So then we, from now on, know no one
according to the flesh" (v. 16a).

"Through glory and dishonor, through evil report and good report; as deceivers and yet true; as unknown and yet well known; as dying and yet behold we live; as being disciplined and yet not being put to death; as made sorrowful yet always rejoicing; as poor yet enriching many; as having nothing and yet possessing all things" (6:8-10).

"For even when we came into Macedonia, our flesh had no rest, but we were afflicted in everything; without were fightings, within were fears" (7:5).

"But I myself, Paul,...in person am base among you, but while absent am bold toward you" (10:1).

"For even if I should boast somewhat more abundantly concerning our authority, which the Lord has given for building you up and not for overthrowing you, I will not be put to shame" (v. 8).

"Because while his letters, someone says, are weighty and strong, his bodily presence is weak and his speech contemptible" (v. 10).

"But I count myself to be inferior to the super-apostles in nothing. But even if I am

3

a layman in speech, yet I am not in knowledge; indeed in every way we have made this manifest in all things to you" (11:5-6).

"And because of the transcendence of the revelations, in order that I might not be exceedingly lifted up, there was given to me a thorn in the flesh, a messenger of Satan, that he might buffet me, in order that I might not be exceedingly lifted up. Concerning this I entreated the Lord three times that it might depart from me. And He has said to me, My grace is sufficient for you, for My power is perfected in weakness. Most gladly therefore I will rather boast in my weaknesses that the power of Christ might tabernacle over me....For when I am weak, then I am powerful" (12:7-9, 10b).

"For the weapons of our warfare are not fleshly but powerful before God for the overthrowing of strongholds" (10:4).

PAUL IN 2 CORINTHIANS

As we read 2 Corinthians carefully before God, we seem to meet two persons—Paul in himself and Paul in Christ. Everything Paul speaks of, from chapter one to chapter thirteen, is all according to this principle. If we summarized Paul's message in this book, we could cover everything with his words in chapter four, "We have this treasure in earthen vessels." In chapter one we see this treasure being put into the earthen vessel. From 3:1 through the end of the book, we see the earthen vessel on the one hand and the treasure on the other hand. After reading these words before God, we spontaneously will see under His enlightenment that the earthen vessel does not hinder the treasure from shining. The earthen vessel does not bury the power of the treasure.

Here we see a person. We have mentioned before that 2 Corinthians is the most personal book in the New Testament. Many Epistles are filled with doctrine, truth, and revelation. Many Epistles move from God's point of view to our point of view. Second Corinthians, however, is the only book in the New Testament which shows us the very kind of person whom God used to pass on His revelation. If we did not have the book of 2 Corinthians, we would never know Paul himself. We would know what he accomplished, but we would never know this ministry. Second Corinthians shows us his ministry, and from his ministry, we meet the man. We see that he was an earthen vessel.

THE IDEAL CHRISTIAN

When I first became a Christian, I had my own concept of the ideal Christian, and I tried my utmost to be that kind of Christian. I thought that if only I could attain to the ideal I had conceived, then I would attain perfection. I wanted to be perfect, but I had my own ideal and standard for being a perfect Christian. I thought that if I could reach this standard, I would be perfect. I thought a perfect Christian should smile from morning to night. If he shed tears, I thought he was not victorious, but a failure. I would even say he was wrong. I thought a perfect Christian should be bold, unafraid, and courageous in every situation. If he was fearful in anything, I would say he did not have faith. I would say he was not perfect because he did not trust in the Lord. I also thought the perfect Christian was never sad. If a person was sad, I doubted that he was perfect. I could mention many other criteria, but I do not need to mention too many of these concepts to you. I believe that many of the younger brothers and sisters have ideals of what a Christian is. I am not criticizing because I used to think the same way myself.

PAUL WAS A MAN

One day I read the passage in 2 Corinthians where Paul was sorrowful. I asked, "Was Paul sorrowful?" I read that he shed many tears. I asked, "Did Paul cry?" I read that Paul suffered and was sad. I asked, "Did Paul suffer, and was he sad?" I read that he was burdened and despaired even of his life. I asked, "Did Paul despair?" As I continued reading, I saw that there were many things of which I had never thought. I had never considered that a person like Paul would have these problems. I began to realize that Christians are not another type of angel. God has not put a race of angels on the earth and said, "These are Christians." I also began to see that Paul was very close to us; he was not so far off. Paul was someone I know; he was not a stranger. I know him because I saw that he was a man.

THE TREASURE MANIFESTED
IN EARTHEN VESSELS

Many people have a concept of an ideal Christian. Please remember that this ideal was created by us, not by God. That kind of ideal Christian does not exist, nor does God want us to be such. Here we meet an earthen vessel, but the special characteristic of this earthen vessel is that a treasure has been put into it. The treasure transcends and overshadows the earthen vessel and manifests itself from within the vessel. This is the meaning of Christianity and of being a Christian. In Paul, we see a man who was afraid yet strong. He was troubled in his heart yet had hope. He was surrounded by enemies yet was not captured. Although he met with persecution, he did not feel rejected or cast aside. He seemingly was knocked down, but he did not die (2 Cor. 4:7-9). We see his weaknesses, but when he was weak, he was powerful (12:10b). We see him bearing about in the body the putting to death of

Jesus, but the life of Jesus was manifested in his body (4:10). We see him being slandered, but he had a good name. He seemingly led others astray, but he was honest. He seemingly was not famous, but everyone knew him. He seemingly was about to die, but he lived. He seemingly was punished, but not unto death. He seemingly was sad, but he always rejoiced. He seemingly was poor, but he made many rich. He seemingly had nothing, but he had everything (6:8-10). This is a real Christian. This is true Christianity.

A Christian is a person in whom there is a basic, but harmonious, paradox. Christianity means having a life in which there is an incomprehensible, spiritual paradox. God gives us this paradox. Some people think there is only a treasure but not an earthen vessel. Others think that the earthen vessel prevents them from going on. Human thought is always so extreme. We think it would be ideal just having the treasure. We think that the earthen vessel prevents us from going on. Before God, however, we see a treasure placed in earthen vessels. The earthen vessel is not destroyed, and it does not frustrate any-thing. The treasure is in the earthen vessel.

GOD'S POWER BEING MANIFESTED IN MAN'S WEAKNESS

The apostle said that he had a thorn in his flesh (2 Cor. 12:7). I do not know what this thorn was, but I know this thorn made Paul weak. He prayed to the Lord about the matter three times, hoping the Lord would remove the thorn. However, the Lord said to him, "My grace is sufficient for you" (vv. 8-9). The Lord said even though the thorn in his flesh made Paul weak, His power was perfected in this weakness. How is the Lord's power perfected in human weakness? He said, "My power will taber-nacle over your weakness," which means "My power will overshadow or cover your weakness." This is Christianity. Christianity does not eliminate weaknesses, nor does it only look to the Lord's power. Christianity means that the Lord's power is manifested in man's weakness. Christianity does not mean that a new race of strange angels is created on the earth. Christianity means that man's weaknesses can manifest God's power.

Let me give an example. Once I had a very serious illness. I was x-rayed three times in two months, and each time the report was very grave. I prayed, I believed, and I hoped that God would cure my illness. At times my strength was greater than normal. Before God, I confessed that I had been empowered, but I was angry because I did not know the reason God was treating me this way. At certain times I would be well and full of strength, but I would relapse without warning. What was the use of God giving me this temporary strength? I was very sick at heart. One day as I was reading the Bible, I came across 2 Corinthians 12. Paul prayed to God three times about that thorn, but the Lord was not willing to do anything. Instead, He said, "My grace is sufficient for you." The Lord increased His grace because of the thorn. The Lord increased His power because of the weakness. I saw what Christianity was. As I lay in bed, I asked the Lord to show me more clearly what this was all about. Inwardly, I had

11

the impression of a boat in a river. The boat required ten feet of water for navigation. In the river, however, a submerged rock rose five feet from the bottom of the river. If the Lord so desired, He could remove the boulder to let the boat pass, but within there was a question: "Would it be better for Me to remove the rock or to increase the water level by five feet?" God asked me if it would be better to remove the boulder or to increase the water level by five feet. I told the Lord that it would be better to increase the water level by five feet.

From that day onward many of my difficulties were gone. I dare not say that I was never tempted again, but praise God, from that matter I discovered God has other ways to meet our needs. This is Christianity. I repeat, Christianity does not remove the boulder; it increases the water level by five feet. This is Christianity. Are there difficulties? Yes, we all have difficulties. Are there trials? Yes, we all are tried. Are there weaknesses? Yes, we all have weaknesses. Please remember one thing, however, that the Lord does not eliminate our weaknesses on the negative side nor give us unwarranted power on the positive side. God's power is manifested in weakness, just as our treasure is in earthen vessels.

THE PARADOXICAL SPIRITUAL LIFE

Today I would like to say that no Christian has an earthen vessel that is earthy enough to prohibit the Lord's treasure from being manifested. No matter how weak we are, remember that the Lord's treasure is manifested in it. Therefore, we see a spiritual paradox in Paul and in us. Do we know what people said about Paul? They said that his speech was contemptible (10:10b), that he took them by guile (12:16), and that he was fickle and said "Yes, yes" and "No, no" (1:17). They said his letters were weighty and strong enough to terrify people (10:9-10). But paradoxically, God's treasure looks very good in such an earthen vessel. God's treasure would not look so nice without the earthen vessel. I am saying that Paul was a genuine man. Thank God that the Lord shined out, or broke out, from within him. He was not a man without feelings. But in his sorrow, he said, "I always rejoice." He was not rejoicing constantly or in sorrow constantly; rather, he constantly rejoiced in his sorrow.

Let me tell you that this is the special characteristic of Christianity. There is a smile while tears are flowing. Many Christians act better than Paul, but they do not live like a Christian. They only can praise the Lord; they are not like a Christian. Many Christians think they can attain a state of never being sorrowful or troubled. There are others who are continually sorrowful and troubled. This means that the treasure has not been expressed in them. But here we have a man through whom the Lord Jesus could pass. I have seen some of the Lord's most outstanding children. When I saw them, I immediately knew who they were and what kind of persons they were. But at the same time I knew what kind of persons they were before the Lord. Today we do not want to see any trace of the earthen vessel when we look at people. Sometimes, however, our eyes only see the earthen vessel. Those who know God, however, are able to see the treasure in earthen vessels when they look at God's children.

Once I met a sister in the Lord. As soon as I met her, I knew that she had a quick disposition. She acted and spoke quickly; she was quick to rebuke others and quick to write letters. Thank the Lord, however, that there were probably one hundred letters in her wastepaper basket which had never been mailed. Because of the earthen vessel, she would write the letters, but the letters in the wastepaper basket proved that she also had the treasure. The treasure was in the earthen vessel. When one saw her, he knew her. She was this kind of person by nature, but one could also see the Lord in her. Sometimes we see a person suffering under trials. But we also see the riches he possesses. This is the treasure in the earthen vessel.

I hope we would see something before the Lord. Today God is not requiring or expecting abstract things. Some brothers ask me why they are so weak. I say that weakness does not matter at all; they will become strong. One brother asked me what he should do after having done a terrible job. I told him that it was not a problem because the important thing is that God puts this treasure into us. We do not need to pretend, by fixing up the earthen vessel. We do not need to cultivate a certain tone or style. Everything comes from God. The treasure can be expressed from within us, the earthen vessels.

I had a conversation with the deacons this last Lord's Day. Many of them said that they were praying for a certain family member, a certain sickness, or a certain matter. I asked them how it was going. They each told me that they believed God would heal their illnesses or save their sons and spouses. They were all very confident, so confident that they did not have the slightest doubt. But we should wait and see. The sick ones are still ill, the sons and spouses are still unrepentant, and the difficult matters still remain. Their kind of faith belongs to the angels, not to earthen vessels. Their faith is too abstract; it is too good. No one in the world has such great faith.

One brother came to tell me that he was learning to believe in God. He dared not say what the outcome would be. Perhaps it would turn out all right, but even if it did not, he would still believe. He prayed to God the day before, and God gave him His promise. He knew that God had answered his prayer, but for some reason he began to doubt when he got up that morning. He prayed again, but he did not know what to do. As he was walking on the road, he began to doubt again, but he did not know what to do. I told him that his doubts were unimportant. True faith cannot be killed by doubts. In fact, real faith looks better when it is surrounded by doubt. I know what I am saying. I hope you will not misunderstand me; I do not want you to go out and doubt. The main point is that our human, earthen vessel is joined to God's treasure. There is not just the latter.

I like reading about the prayer of the early church for Peter to be freed from the hands of evil men. God heard their prayer. When Peter returned to the house and knocked on the door, they said that it must be his angel (Acts 12:12-15). Do we see that this is faith, real faith? God heard the prayers, but human weakness was in it.

17

We do not see them doing anything to hide their weaknesses. Some people today have greater faith than those in the house of Mary and Mark. They are so certain that God will send an angel and break the lock on the prison doors. Perhaps they are like those in the examples we gave on the Lord's Day. If the wind blows, they say it is Peter knocking. If the rain strikes the house, they say Peter is knocking. These people have such great faith, but what they believe does not happen. Let me say frankly: This kind of Christian can only do things by himself and cheat a group of gullible people. Those who know God will say that there is an earthen vessel in Christianity. In Christianity the treasure is in earthen vessels. Human doubt is really an abomination, and it is sin. Nothing that comes from the earthen vessel alone can be accepted. The crucial matter is not the earthen vessel, but the fact that a treasure has been placed in it. We do not need to improve or fix the earthen vessel. The treasure has been placed into the vessel.

Many times we have the assurance that

God has heard our prayer. During the moments when we feel that our faith is strongest, we may also sense the presence of doubts. When we hear God's voice most clearly, we will also hear the devil's voice. In this kind of situation, I thank and praise God for the faith He has given us. This faith cannot change; it is still present. Before God we can see that the treasure is all the time expressed through the earthen vessel. God's glory is manifested through the earthen vessel.

Many Christians have a life and walk that are all too artificial; they do not express the treasure. These ones only have human endeavor, performance, and outward behavior. A normal Christian life, however, is one in which one may doubt even in the moments of his greatest assurance. It is one in which one finds himself inwardly weak even in the moments of his greatest strength, inwardly fearful in the midst of real courage before God, and inwardly doubting in the moments of exhilarating joy. This kind of paradox proves that the treasure is in the earthen vessel.

HUMAN WEAKNESS
NOT LIMITING GOD'S POWER

Finally, I would like to say that I especially thank God because no human weakness can limit God's power. What do we think in our hearts? We tend to think that if there is sorrow, there should not be joy; if there are tears, there should not be praise; if there is weakness, there should not be power; if there is pressing on every side, there should be constriction; if there is casting down, there should be destruction; and if there are doubts, we should be unable to believe. But tonight I would like to loudly declare that this is not true. God wants us to arrive at the point where we see that everything human is just an earthen vessel to contain God's treasure. Everything human is an earthen vessel for God's treasure. Nothing human is able to bury God's treasure. We do not need to be disappointed when we meet with disappointment. Although we cannot make it, we should allow something positive to come in, and when it does, it shines better, more brightly, and more gloriously. Many times we have doubts after praying, and we think that everything is finished. When faith comes, however, it magnifies the treasure despite the lingering presence of doubt. Faith makes the treasure more glorious. I am not speaking of an ideal; I know what I am saying. God's treasure can be expressed in earthen vessels. This is a spiritual paradox; it is precious to every Christian. It is in the context of this spiritual paradox that we live and learn to know our God.

As we journey along this way, we will discover the immensity of the spiritual contradiction that exists within us. As time goes on, we find this cleavage, this dividing gulf, is ever widening; the contradiction within us is ever accentuated. At the same time, the treasure is expressed ever clearer. The earthen vessel remains an earthen vessel. How wonderful this picture is! We find a man whose original traits remain intact, yet God gives him a patience far more excellent than his natural resilience. It is better to see a man in whom God has placed humility than to see a naturally reticent person. It is better to see a man in whom God has placed meekness than to see a person who is weak and impotent by nature. It is better to see a person in whom God's power resides than to see a naturally strong man. The inward difference is enormous. It matters little what kind of earthen vessel we have; the treasure can always go inside. The earthen vessel remains an earthen vessel, but it is now a filled vessel. All weak people think that they are too earthen; their vessels are too full of clay and they are without any hope. Please remember that we have no reason to be disappointed or troubled. Whatever is spiritual, strong, powerful, and comes from the Lord can be manifested in us and will shine brighter and be magnified through the earthen vessel. Since this is the case, we can see the importance of the treasure.

Brothers and sisters, everything depends upon the treasure. I must repeat, all situations revolve around this matter. Every outcome is positive. Those whose eyes are on the negative things are fools. The Lord can express Himself through everyone. When we have the treasure, many will know it.